PUTTING
IT ALL
T*GETHER

A Prophetic Overview of The End Times

HAROLD V. NICKEL

Quotations from the Old and New Testament are taken from the Authorized King James Version of the Holy Bible.

Cover illustration incorporates
The Four Horsemen of the Apocalypse
by Albrecht Dürer

TABLE OF CONTENTS

INTRODUCTION

There is much preaching on prophecy today. Many prophecy books have been written over the years and new ones appear on the bookstore shelves regularly.

The maze of information makes confusion possible especially in the sequence of prophetic events. Uniformity of thought prevails among many Bible scholars concerning certain major occurrences and their order in the prophetic spectrum. Not alone is it important to understand these events but also to see them in their succession.

This is the purpose for PUTTING IT ALL TOGETHER. In this book there is little attempt at treatise. Rather, the reader is presented with a concise, easy to understand, "bird's eye" view of the prophetic scene. Beginning at the Incarnation, each major event relating to the person and work of Christ is highlighted in a brief manner and scripturally documented. It is hoped that this short book, a synoptic, will stimulate a desire for further study of prophetic truth. If this is the result, the author's effort shall have been duly rewarded.

The Author

IN APPRECIATION

Appreciation is expressed to my family for their assistance in the original publication in 1975: Ray for editing; Beverly and Randy for cover design and artwork; and Rosalie, my wife, for typing. And now a further word of appreciation extends to Beverly for a new cover design and assistance in making this reprint a reality.

1

DEITY IN DUST

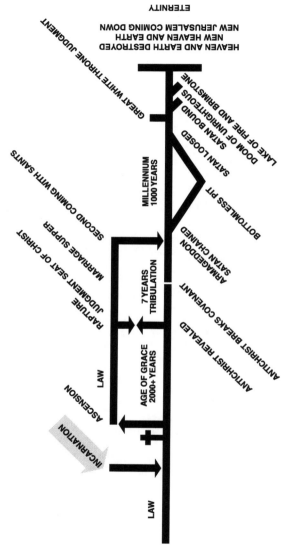

LAW

INCARNATION

ASCENSION

LAW

AGE OF GRACE
2000+ YEARS

RAPTURE

JUDGMENT SEAT OF CHRIST

MARRIAGE SUPPER

SECOND COMING WITH SAINTS

7 YEARS
TRIBULATION

ANTICHRIST REVEALED

ANTICHRIST BREAKS COVENANT

ARMAGEDDON
SATAN CHAINED

BOTTOMLESS PIT

MILLENNIUM
1000 YEARS

SATAN LOOSED

DOOM OF UNRIGHTEOUS

LAKE OF FIRE AND BRIMSTONE

GREAT WHITE THRONE JUDGMENT

HEAVEN AND EARTH DESTROYED
NEW HEAVEN AND EARTH
NEW JERUSALEM COMING DOWN

ETERNITY

THE WORD BECAME FLESH

And the Word was made flesh and dwelt among us.
John 1:14

The day is far spent and night comes on. In the distance are the lights of the little town. The journey has been long and tiring for many and particularly so for one who is about to be delivered of a child. The lights in the distance bring hope—hope for a good night's sleep in one of the rooms of the town's only inn. And so the pilgrims press on.

Such probably was the experience of Joseph and Mary. What a disappointment it must have been when they were informed that there was no room in the inn. Only one choice remained, bed down with the animals. Not a pleasant thought, I'm sure, but what else was there, and besides they were very tired.

I can imagine that Joseph had been sleeping for a time when all of a sudden he hears someone speaking softly to him. It's Mary, and her voice carries an anxious note. "Honey, I can't sleep. I think it's going to happen tonight. What do we do?" He probably responds as any first time, prospective father would respond. "You're what? Not really! Not tonight!"

Leaving conjecture, we go to the actual account of the event in Scripture that reads, "And she brought forth her first-born son, and wrapped him in swaddling clothes, and laid him in a manger, because there was no room for them in the inn" (Luke 2:7).

It is certainly reasonable to assume that in preparing Joseph for this event, the Angel of the Lord had reminded him of the words of Isaiah, the prophet, informing that Mary was that virgin of whom the prophet had spoken, and therefore that child to be born would be "Immanuel"—"God with us" (Isa. 7:14; Matt. 1:18-25).

This prophetic truth of the Old Testament fulfilled at the first coming of Christ is referred to as the Incarnation. Not in this life will this truth ever be fully comprehended and appreciated. Believe it, however, we must for upon it hinges the only hope for a lost and sinning humanity.

The apostle Paul, writing to the church at Galatia, states that "when the fullness of time was come, God sent forth his son" (Gal. 4:4). Somewhere and at some time in eternity past, in the council chambers of an eternal God, this event, it would seem, was planned by a triune God. What transpired there we are left only to speculate. All we are told is that an event, one that would present Deity in dust, slated to happen at a certain point in time, would be accomplished by this first coming of our Lord and Savior, Jesus Christ.

The earliest prophetic reference to this event takes us back to the beginning, to a pristine garden setting, in the form of a promise. That beautiful setting had been brought to chaos by Satan and sin. To restore that original scene there came the promise of a redeemer: "And I will put enmity between thee and the woman and between thy seed and her seed; he shall bruise thy head, and thou shalt bruise his heel" (Gen. 3:15).

While this promise seems somewhat vague and offers little detail as to it's out-working, that which follows in the Scriptures—first in type and shadow (Gen. 3:21; Ex. 12:12&13), then in the prophet's message (Isa. 53; 9:6&7; Micah 5:2), and finally in the actual event (Matt. 1:18-23; Luke 2:30-33)—leaves no question about the prophetic significance of this promise.

As we view the prophetic scheme, this is where it must begin. John, the beloved disciple, puts it this way, "In the beginning was the Word, and the Word was with God, and the Word was God.... And the word was made flesh, and dwelt among us and we beheld his glory, the glory as of the only begotten of the Father, full of grace and truth" (John 1:1&14).

Among the many references to this truth in the Scriptures, there is one by the apostle Paul, who writes, "Who, being in the form of God, thought it not robbery to be equal with God, but made himself of no reputation, and took upon him the form of a servant, and was made in the likeness of men; and, being found in fashion as a man, he humbled himself and became obedient unto death, even the death of the cross. Wherefore, God also hath highly exalted him, and given him a name which is above every name, that at the name of Jesus every knee should bow, of things in heaven, and things in earth, and things under the earth, and that every tongue should confess that Jesus Christ is Lord, to the glory of God, the Father" (Phil. 2:6-11).

God's method of accomplishing the out-working of his promise, to which reference in the Scriptures is replete, was that of the Incarnation. Jesus Christ, the eternal Word, God manifested in the flesh, both Son of God and Son of Man; this is incomprehensible prophetic truth fulfilled!

Christ's death on the cross made good the promise of God to that world lost through Adam's fall. The promise of redemption was—not only in its ultimate for the total world as such, but more importantly to us—for you and me personally. His resurrection, of course, vindicated the fact that he was God and his now exalted state presently remains the guarantee for the total of that redemption which predicated the Incarnation in the first instance.

In conclusion it must be underscored again that this truth of the Incarnation will never be either fully comprehended or understood by any this side of eternity. However, it must be believed and to this extent it can be understood and appreciated. In its simplest statement, the apostle Paul states it this way, "God was in Christ reconciling the world unto himself" (II Cor. 5:19). We are that world and to that world echo the words of the Savior himself as they come ringing down the corridor of time: "For God so loved the world, that he gave his only begotten son, that whosoever believeth in him should not perish, but have everlasting life" (John 3:16).

2

OUT OF SIGHT

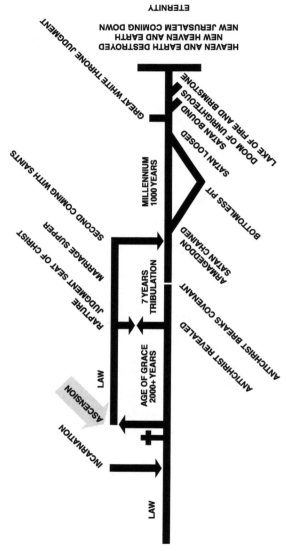

CAUGHT UP INTO GLORY

Ye men of Galilee, why stand ye gazing into heaven?
This same Jesus, who is taken up from you into heaven,
shall so come in like manner as ye have seen him go
into heaven.

Acts 1:11

Several men—young men, many believe—had been chosen by Christ to become his disciples. Various vocations in life had been theirs. For approximately three years now they had been in close association with their Master. They had watched him heal the sick, raise the dead and cast out demons. They had heard his discourses.

The fond hope of the kingdom foretold by the prophets of Israel had been theirs, one which had become more and more real as the months and years passed. Associated with this, of course, were their personal aspirations. The thought of a possible delay in the realization of all of this had not occurred to these dedicated and committed young followers of the Galilean. Then came the "shocker," an incredible announcement by their Master, that he would be apprehended by his own people's leaders and crucified!

The reaction, as would be expected, was a natural one. Frustration, disillusionment, despair are words which could best describe their feelings. One can only imagine the thoughts that must have flooded the minds of these devoted followers of the Christ. The reaction of Peter is seen a bit later as he says, "I go fishing." He did, too, but caught nothing (John 21:3). Matthew, though nowhere stated, must have thought of his former vocation, that of collecting revenue for the Roman government. It at the least offered financial security. In like manner, James and John probably relived their experience of leaving their father alone mending the nets for another fishing expedition. His possible reluctance to let them go was now perhaps a vivid memory. Such, no doubt, could describe the setting. To these disciples it was now a hopeless situation, I'm sure.

It seems common to experience that it is always the darkest just before the dawn. But then the darkness begins to dispel as the rays of morning light bear upon it until finally it is completely replaced by the brilliance of a new day. Such was the progressively unfolding experience of these discouraged, disheartened disciples. That darkness, however, that had invaded their lives was meant to be dispelled by the "morning light" words of their Master—words that are immortal. What words! "Let not your heart be troubled; ye believe in God, believe also in me. In my Father's house are many mansions; if it were not so, I would have told you. I go to prepare a place for you. And if I go and prepare a place of you, I will come again, and receive you unto myself, that where I am, there ye may be also. And where I go ye know, and the way ye know. Thomas saith unto him, Lord, we know not where thou goest; and how can we know the way? Jesus saith unto him, I am the way, the truth and the life; no man cometh unto the Father, but by me" (Jn14:1-6).

It is done! Sin and Satan have done their dastardly deed. Christ has been crucified. Redemption's price has been paid for a lost world. Joseph of Arimathaea and Nicodemus have begged the body of Jesus. It has been placed in the former's own unused tomb. Moreover, three days have passed. But then the darkness gives way to morning light! News of the resurrection breaks upon Jerusalem and its environs! Each gospel writer records the story in his own unique style to document the most important fact of the Gospel and of history.

The gospel fact with its associated truths is summed up by the apostle Paul in his letter to the Corinthian believers as follows: "Moreover, brethren, I declare unto you the gospel which I preached unto you, which also ye have received and in which ye stand; by which also ye are saved....that Christ died for our sins according to the scriptures; and that he was buried, and that he rose again the third day according to the scriptures; and that he was seen of Cephas, then of the twelve" (I Cor.15:1-5).

Forty days have passed (Acts 2:3). Little is recorded about those days. It would be safe to assume that they were days of teaching. Judging from Dr. Luke's account in the opening words of Acts we may be sure that some instruction concerned the hope for the kingdom which had occupied these disciples and most probably had motivated them to follow the Master in the first place (Acts 1:6-8).

This account directs us to the Mount of Olives, a place not unfamiliar to the Savior's presence. He is there with his disciples. An exciting event is imminent. He had made reference to it in those hours prior to the cross but they had not comprehended it (John 14:2,3). There come from his lips those last minute instructions to these men who had been by his side through it all—that is, almost all. Then suddenly, "And when he had spoken these things, while they beheld, he was taken up, and a cloud received him out of their sight. And while they looked steadfastly toward heaven as he went up, behold, two men stood by them in white apparel; who also said, ye men of Galilee, why stand ye gazing up into heaven? This same Jesus, who is taken up from you into heaven, shall so come in like manner as ye have seen him go into heaven" (Acts 1:9-11). Now they were beginning to understand.

Jesus had told these followers, "I go...I will come again" (John 14:2,3). Now the angel said, "This same Jesus who is taken up from you into heaven shall so come in like manner as ye have seen him go" (Acts 1:11).

It would seem that nothing has happened since for nearly two thousand years, but his program has not been at a standstill. True, he hasn't returned. However, this imminent event does appear to be very near at hand. More will be said about that later. What is important is that much has and continues to happen.

He told his disciples that he would "prepare a place for them" (John 14:3). There is no reason to doubt his occupation with this. He promised to send the Comforter, the

Holy Spirit (John 14:16-18, 26; 16:7). The Acts of the Apostles records the fulfillment of this promise (Acts 1:8, 2:1-11). His purpose is to call out of this world a people for himself during his absence. He himself coined the term applied to that people when he said, "I will build my church" (Matt. 16:18). He's still doing this.

John, the beloved, writing about that church in its infant years, gives a further picture of the Savior's activity now and over the intervening time since he made his exit into the clouds. The ideal for the believer, of course, is not to sin but John knew, as we know all too well, that idealism and reality are often far apart. Thus the words, "My little children, if any man sin, we have an advocate with the Father, Jesus Christ, the righteous; And he is the propitiation for our sins, and not for ours only, but also for the sins of the whole world" I John 2:2). Having been caught up into glory, he desires to be your advocate but only if you wish him to be. We all need one, to be sure!

3

TRANSCENDING SPACE

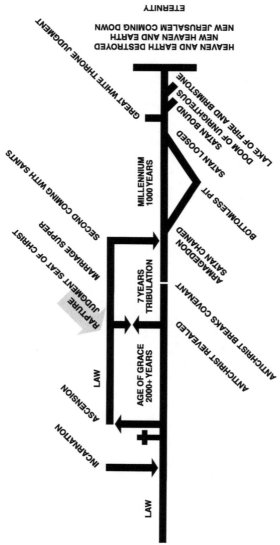

UNTO THEM THAT LOOK FOR HIM

*And unto them that look for him shall he appear the
second time without sin unto salvation.*

Hebrews 9:28

An event which is imminent awaits every born-again child
of God. Suddenly, and we believe soon, an entire generation of believers will disappear from planet earth. They
will be taken into the presence of Christ at his coming.
This has been and continues to be the hope that buoys up
the believer on the sea of life however violent the storm
may rage (I Thess. 4:18).

A small colony of believers existed in Thessalonica.
They had been instructed by the apostle Paul about the
return of Christ and they, as he, seemed to be living in an
attitude of expectancy. It appears, however, that they had
not taken into account a fact of life, that of dying. In the
passage of time some of their number had passed away.
The result was one of disillusion and question on the part
of the bereaved.

These believers had, of course, expected to meet
the Lord together. Now the logical concern was would
those who had experienced death be "short changed" by

missing this glorious event? This occasioned the words of the apostle: "But I would not have you to be ignorant, brethren, concerning them who are asleep, that ye sorrow not, even as others who have no hope. For if we believe that Jesus died and rose again, even so them also who sleep in Jesus will God bring with him. For this we say unto you by the word of the Lord, that we who are alive and remain unto the coming of the Lord shall not precede them who are asleep. For the Lord himself shall descend from heaven with a shout, with the voice of the archangel, and with the trump of God; and the dead in Christ shall rise first; Then we who are alive and remain shall be caught up together with them in the clouds, to meet the Lord in the air; and so shall we ever be with the Lord. Wherefore, comfort one another with these words" (I Thess. 4:13-18).

What a blessing has resulted from the anxiety of those early believers at Thessalonica for believers through the succeeding generations. Without it, these immortal words of the apostle might not have been penned. We would possibly have remained ignorant of the events associated with this phase of Christ's coming again. Let us consider some of these events.

A study of the Scriptures will reveal that over the years God has dealt with man in various ways, in different eras, commonly referred to as dispensations. The present one is that of Grace which has now extended for nearly two thousand years.

When this present era of Grace has run its course, the One who said, "I will come again" (John 14:3), will descend personally from Heaven to which he was taken. His glorious, personal return will be heralded and accompanied by "a shout, the voice of the archangel, and with the trump of God" (I Thess. 4:16). Most important, his return will be personal. The believer looks, in reality, not just for an event, but also for a person—The Person! "The Lord himself shall descend" (I Thess. 4:16)!

Christ's return will leave the world with an unexplainable mystery. But for the believer it will be an exciting, triumphant change from mortality to immortality (I Cor. 15:54). No longer will mystery prevail for the believer, for then "we shall know even as we have been fully known" (I Cor. 13:12).

What relief must have come to those bereaved of their loved ones when they learned that "the dead in Christ shall rise first" (I Thess. 4:16). It would seem that those who have experienced death are to have a head start and "then we who are alive and remain shall be caught up together with them in the clouds, to meet the Lord in the air" (I Thess. 4:17).

Those who have meant so much to us in this life will be there. There's no mistake about it. Neither will they miss out on anything. They will rise first and we'll join them in being "caught up to meet the Lord in the air" (I Thess. 4:17). Our experiences with the icy hand of death will fast fade into oblivion in the reunion that awaits us in the presence of the Lord himself.

Reunions with loved ones in this life, however blessed, are most frequently short-lived and marred by tearful partings. Not so with this event for we read, "so shall we ever be with the Lord" (I Thess. 4:17). The ones whose places have been emptied here below shall once more be by our side, but this time forever.

Most important, we will meet the Lord himself! He made it all possible. We have seen him through the eye of faith only. Here "we shall see him as he is" (I John 3:2) and "ever be with the Lord" (I Thess. 4:18).

This event is an imminent one. The scene today predicates the belief that it is very near. Such truths as have been here considered will either bring fear or offer comfort. To the believer they offer comfort: "Wherefore comfort one another with these words" (I Thess. 4:18).

"Unto them that look for him shall he appear the second time without sin unto salvation" (Heb. 9:28). Are you among those looking for him?

4

CHAOS AND CATACLYSM

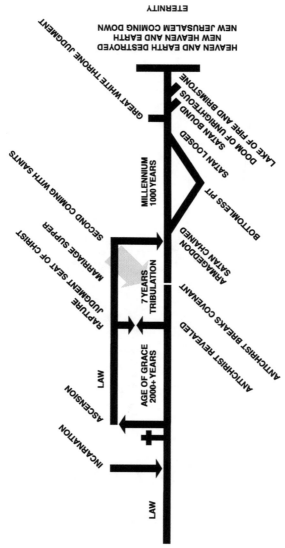

ETERNITY

HEAVEN AND EARTH DESTROYED
NEW HEAVEN AND EARTH
NEW JERUSALEM COMING DOWN

GREAT WHITE THRONE JUDGMENT

SATAN BOUND
DOOM OF UNRIGHTEOUS
LAKE OF FIRE AND BRIMSTONE

SATAN LOOSED

MILLENNIUM
1000 YEARS

BOTTOMLESS PIT

ARMAGEDDON
SATAN CHAINED

SECOND COMING WITH SAINTS

7 YEARS
TRIBULATION

ANTICHRIST BREAKS COVENANT

RAPTURE
JUDGMENT SEAT OF CHRIST
MARRIAGE SUPPER

ANTICHRIST REVEALED

LAW

AGE OF GRACE
2000+ YEARS

ASCENSION

INCARNATION

LAW

ON EARTH, TRIBULATION

For then shall be great tribulation, such as was not since the beginning of the world to this time, no, or ever shall be.

Matthew 24:21

The world goes on. It only takes three days for one who has died to be buried and, for the most part, forgotten. So it will be when suddenly and mysteriously an entire generation of believers has vanished from this world's scene.

While bedlam will prevail initially, the behind-the-scene, organized forces of Antichrist will be swiftly marshaled into action, neutralizing initial shock. Educators, scientists and left-behind liberal preachers will offer needed explanation to satisfy a deluded world. Major devastation caused by the sudden vanishing of a small minority from this planet will quickly be repaired and the world will go on. Or will it?

It would appear that all is well on planet earth for a time to follow but not so as events unfold. In fact, no dark period of this world's history will compare with that for which this world is headed. Jesus referred to this when he stated, "except those days should be shortened there should no flesh be saved" (Matt. 24:22). As the events of this coming period are examined, it would almost seem that God will turn it all over to Satan, saying, "You've always wanted to run this world. It's all yours now. Try your hand at it. The people who have believed me are no longer around to hinder (I Thess. 4:13-18). My presence in the person of the Holy Spirit will no longer restrain you (II Thess. 2:7). You've wanted your chance. Here it is." While such may not actually transpire, it does, nevertheless, describe the setting in a measure.

The apostle Paul informs the believers at Thessalonica that this period cannot begin before certain things happen. Among these is the removal of the hindering force now operative. The reference, we believe, is to the Holy Spirit, who, when the church or the body of Christ, composed of all born-again believers in Jesus Christ, has been raptured, will also be taken up out of this world. Thus Satan will not be hindered as he is today by the active ministry and power of the Holy Spirit (II Thess. 2:7).

The saints (believers in Christ, Eph. 1:1) have been raptured; the Holy Spirit has been removed and Satan the great Usurper, seizes authority over a world that he has long been preparing for this hour. To this world he sends a leader—a sinister one, the Antichrist—who has both the charisma to capture its loyalty and the aspiration to rule over it (II Thess. 2:3-10; Dan. 7:24; Rev. 13:1).

Other events that mark this period deserve mention. There will be an invasion of Israel by northern forces. These are believed to be Russia and her allies. Devastating defeat is predicted for the invading army (Ez. 38, 39).

There is further recorded the sudden and complete destruction and annihilation of both spiritual and political Babylon. Many believe this to refer to a worldwide religious system and an end-time political entity. Both meet their doom by God's special fiat (Rev. 17, 18; Jer. 53).

A covenant is to be negotiated between Antichrist and Israel. It will probably be designed to provide protection for the tiny nation. The covenant is made only to be brutally broken later by Antichrist (Dan. 9:27) who receives his power and authority from Satan himself (Rev. 13:2). This accounts for his actions.

The book of Revelation details some most terrible and indescribable events (Rev. 6-19). They beggar description for any with even the most vivid imagination.

The culmination of all will be at Armageddon. This possibly could be World War III. This encounter will result in a blood bath which will make the other great wars of history appear as child's play by any comparison (Rev. 14:14-21; 19:17-21).

All these events and more will comprise the fast-moving drama during a seven-year period. This period is referred to as the Seventieth Week of Daniel's prophecy, a "week" of 7 years (Dan. 9:24-27). Its drama will particularly unfold during the latter half of this era. Christ refers to this portion of the "week" of years as a time of "great tribulation" (Matt. 24:21).

As stated previously, we are told by Christ that those days have necessarily been shortened (Matt. 24:22). Both their beginning and their ending are marked—the beginning by or near by the coming of Christ FOR his saints (I Thess. 4:13-18) and the ending by his coming WITH his saints and the subsequent inauguration of his kingdom (Rev. 1:7; Jude 14, 15).

While events on earth have been moving in their predicted course during this period, the believer has been with Christ. He has been judged, literally manifested or reviewed at the Judgment Seat of Christ (II Cor. 5:10). He has either been rewarded or he has suffered loss (I Cor. 3:11-15). He has been royally dined at the wedding feast, the Marriage Supper of the Lamb (Rev. 19:7). Further, it is most reasonable to assume and believe that he has been presented assignment of responsibility in the administration of the coming kingdom in this world under the reign of King Jesus (I Cor. 6:2; Matt. 25:21).

Judging the world scene by those events that the Scriptures tell us will introduce the tribulation era, we may well conclude that this period is imminently near. If such a conclusion is indeed valid—and we certainly believe that it is—then those who read these pages face a choice. It is an election for king and kingdom. The choice is for Christ and his kingdom or for that of Antichrist and eternal doom.

To choose Christ brings a hope which will result in meeting Christ in the air and being forever with him. It will mean enjoying all the benefits of his kingdom for eternity. To reject Christ is to be without hope. To such, when Christ returns for his own, it will mean submission in this present world to the rule of Antichrist. Both he and his kingdom are doomed, as are all who reject Christ in this life, to eternal consignment to the "lake which burneth with fire and brimstone" (Rev. 20:15; 21:8).

It is true that many will be saved during the reign of Antichrist through the preaching ministry of 144,000 Jews who will be gloriously converted and become evangelists to the world (Rev. 7). Such faith, however, will probably result in physical death. Also, it is doubtful that any who have had the opportunity to be saved during this present age of Grace—and have rejected Christ—will have another occasion to elect for Christ during this tribulation period (II Cor. 6:2; II Thess. 2:11).

Today is your election day! For whom do you vote— Christ or Antichrist?

5

THE KING
IS COMING

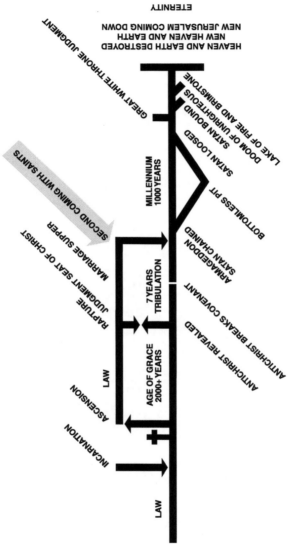

ETERNITY

HEAVEN AND EARTH DESTROYED
NEW HEAVEN AND EARTH
NEW JERUSALEM COMING DOWN

GREAT WHITE THRONE JUDGMENT

SATAN BOUND
DOOM OF UNRIGHTEOUS
LAKE OF FIRE AND BRIMSTONE

SATAN LOOSED

MILLENNIUM
1000 YEARS

BOTTOMLESS PIT

SECOND COMING WITH SAINTS

ARMAGEDDON
SATAN CHAINED

RAPTURE
JUDGMENT SEAT OF CHRIST
MARRIAGE SUPPER

7 YEARS
TRIBULATION

ANTICHRIST BREAKS COVENANT

LAW

ASCENSION

AGE OF GRACE
2000+ YEARS

ANTICHRIST REVEALED

INCARNATION

LAW

EVERY EYE SHALL SEE HIM

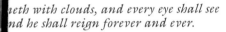

...eth with clouds, and every eye shall see
...nd he shall reign forever and ever.

Revelation 1:7; 11:15

...f Old Testament prophecy is with Israel's
...esented as her Redeemer, Deliverer, and

...of the New Testament message is that the
...t is the Messiah. His rejection is a fact of
...d secular. The kingdom role of Messiah,
...t fulfilled. Both the Old and New Testa-
...is role and obviously since it hasn't been
...future. The minute and detailed fulfill-
...ophet's predictions concerning Messiah
...us Christ leave no doubt concerning his

...ording to prophetic prediction, will extend
...cient people to whom the promise was
...made ready for it through the miss-rule of
...onsequent judgment of God upon it.
...ord millennium itself is not used in the
...t and is that span of time—one thousand

31

years—during which the present world shall enjoy the glorious reign of the Son of God (Rev. 20:7; Isa. 9:7). What we must understand is that Christ's rule will be this world's last and final. It will climax "time." It will be the forerunner to eternity. But more than this, his rule extends into eternity, into that world which supersedes this present world. Thus, his reign is correctly designated as extending forever.

As the stupendous details of the Tribulation stagger the most vivid imagination, so the glorious truths associated with the Millennium boggle the human intellect. It is simply impossible in our world as we know it to comprehend conditions as they will be under the rule of King Jesus. As has been stated before, we can only believe God and leave the details with him.

All of that which is associated with this era is worthy of note, but only a few items shall be mentioned here. While the Scripture indicates that the coming of Christ for his saints at the Rapture will transpire without the world seeing him, that is not so when he returns with his saints to assume the reins of government in this world. We are informed that "every eye shall see him" (Rev. 1:7). I believe Paul, the apostle, refers to this, pointing out that his return will be in two phases. First mentioned is "the blessed hope," that is, the Rapture; and then, "the glorious appearing," the Revelation or unveiling (Titus 2:13). The two are separated by an undisclosed period of time, certainly that of the tribulation period.

It is most difficult to imagine what it would be like in this world without the presence of Satan. Such, though, we are informed will be the experience of the millennium (Rev. 20:1-3). Although he'll no longer dog the steps of man that sinful nature possessed by man will still remain. Not stimulated by Satan's attack, man will no doubt be more prone to submit to the rule of Christ.

Man's inhumanity to man, particularly characterized in the rule of tyrants and the wars of history, will give way to world peace and tranquility (Isa. 2:4; Micah 4:3). Nature, too, shall be tamed as the wild beast and reptile become domesticated, no longer fearing man nor feared by him (Isa. 11:6-9).

True morality only abounds where the knowledge of God exists. In a culture void of that knowledge, man will set his own code by which to live and such will be tempered by the circumstances that surround him. Sin and Satan play their role in those circumstances. Except for hindrance by a sinful heart, it is safe to assume that true morality associated with the knowledge of God will be man's experience around the world. For it is written that "the earth shall be full of the knowledge of the Lord, as the waters cover the sea" (Isa. 11:9).

One of the disciples questioned the Lord in regard to how to pray. In the model prayer that followed come the words, "Thy kingdom come. Thy will be done, as in heaven, so in earth" (Luke 11:2). This prayer of the centuries will yet be answered as the "kingdom of this world is become the kingdom of our Lord, and of his Christ, and he shall reign forever and ever" (Rev. 11:15).

6

COURTROOM OF DEITY

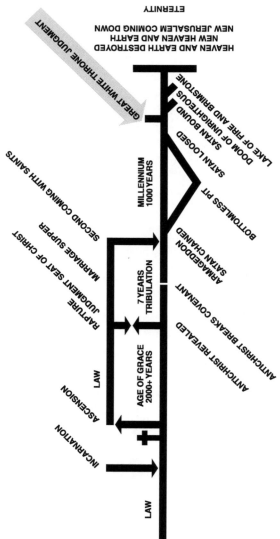

ETERNITY

HEAVEN AND EARTH DESTROYED
NEW HEAVEN AND EARTH
NEW JERUSALEM COMING DOWN

GREAT WHITE THRONE JUDGMENT

SATAN BOUND
DOOM OF UNRIGHTEOUS
LAKE OF FIRE AND BRIMSTONE

SATAN LOOSED

MILLENNIUM
1000 YEARS

BOTTOMLESS PIT

SECOND COMING WITH SAINTS

ARMAGEDDON
SATAN CHAINED

7 YEARS
TRIBULATION

ANTICHRIST BREAKS COVENANT

RAPTURE
JUDGMENT SEAT OF CHRIST
MARRIAGE SUPPER

ANTICHRIST REVEALED

AGE OF GRACE
2000+ YEARS

LAW

ASCENSION

INCARNATION

LAW

AFTER THIS THE JUDGMENT

And I saw a great white throne, and him that sat on it, from whose face the earth and heaven fled away and there was found no place for them.

Revelation 20:11

There are two things, we are told, that cannot be avoided—taxes and death. Yet there are those who have and will escape both.

All sorts of tax evasion schemes have been devised and uncovered and others, I'm sure, will yet be in the future. Death cannot be so avoided. Yet there is a record on file for two who did indeed miss their appointment with death.

Both Enoch and Elijah escaped death (Gen. 5:24; II Kings 2:11). They became the type of that generation of believers in Christ who shall suddenly, mysteriously—and we believe soon—be transplanted from this world into the presence of Christ at the Rapture.

There is one appointment, however, that none will escape. It is the judgment. Whether rich or poor, small or great, all alike will stand to be judged. Paul, the apostle, states it in short terse words, "So, then, every one of us shall give account of himself to God" (Rom. 14:12).

The believer, as mentioned previously, will stand before the Judgment Seat of Christ (II Cor. 5:10) and the unbeliever before the Great White Throne (Rev. 20:11). We are occupied in this chapter with the latter.

The world has enjoyed the rule of King Jesus for a millennium. Satan has been chained and man, one would think, would never lend himself to rebellious plotting against the rule of Christ. On the contrary!

Satan, we are told, is loosed for a season (Rev. 20:7). Man, having a fallen nature, becomes his easy target and prey. Both the result and its climax are best told by John, the Revelator, who states, "And when the thousand years are ended, Satan shall be loosed out of his prison, and shall go out to deceive the nations which are in the four quarters of the earth, Gog and Magog, to gather them together to battle; the number of whom is as the sand of the sea. And they went up on the breadth of the earth, and compassed the camp of the saints about, and the beloved city; and fire came down from God out of heaven, and devoured them. And the devil that deceived them was cast into the lake of fire and brimstone, where the beast and the false prophet are, and shall be tormented day and night forever and ever" (Rev. 20:7-10).

In the very next verse we are ushered into the court-room of Deity. The scene is that of judgment. John further writes with inspired pen: "And I saw a great white throne, and him that sat on it from whose face the earth and the heaven fled away, and there was found no place for them. And I saw the dead, small and great, stand before God, and the books were opened; and another book was opened which is the book of life. And the dead were judged out of those things which were written in the books, according to their works. And the sea gave up the dead that were in it, and death and hades delivered up the dead that were in them; and they were judged every man according to their works. And death and hades were cast into the lake of fire. This is the second death. And whosoever was not found written in the book of life was cast into the lake of fire" (Rev. 20:11-15).

Aspirations toward greatness have occupied many over the centuries. Not the many, only a few in each generation make good their goal. The majority live and die in the class of the ordinary. Whether small or great, however, all the dead, we are informed, stand before the God of the universe. It would appear that difference between smallness and greatness that existed in this life will have been narrowed to nothingness at this point in time. Greatness counted once but no longer. Things will have changed.

In the sophisticated business world of today, records and books are not only a valuable asset but also an absolute, indispensible necessity. For the honorable they are an asset in maintaining and proving legitimacy. Not infrequently, however, records and books are found to be inaccurate as a result of human error or, in some instances, as a result of tampering.

Not so with the books opened there on the edge of time and brink of eternity. The keeper of the records is perfect—he is God himself. No human error or tampering there! Each will meet an accurately detailed record of his own life. This record will be the basis of judgment.

One book, of course, stands out—it is the Book of Life (Rev. 20:15). Both here and elsewhere in Scripture it is God's register of the redeemed. Contrary to the thinking of many who see only the unredeemed appear at this scene of judgment, the very language itself indicates that there will be present those whose names have been written "in the Book of Life." Could this perhaps be the redeemed of the tribulation period and those coming into vital relationship with Christ during the millennium? No amount of conjecture could settle the issue, but conceivably it might be such or even the redeemed of other dispensations. Whatever, we will know then for we will be there with him when it happens.

Death knocking at the door of the residence of the soul is rarely a welcome guest. There is something worse, however. It is called the second death and is synonymous with "the lake of fire." It awaits those departing this life who failed in tending to the matter of registry in the Book of Life. Among them will be the wealthy as well as the poor, the kind and the cruel, the simple and the intellectual, the religious and the profane, the white, black, red and yellow.

The books have been opened, judgment has been rendered, sentence has been passed. Though it is not stated, it is conceivable that the angels could perhaps be dispatched to implement the outcome of this judgment for we read, "And death and hades were cast into the lake of fire. This is the second death. And whosoever was not found written in the book of life was cast into the lake of fire" (Rev. 20:14, 15).

Thus we are brought to the end of "time." For upon the judgment pronounced come the words, "And I saw a new heaven and a new earth" (Rev. 21:1).

Time is fragile. It should be handled carefully. For you and for me it is, at best, short. And it is ours only once to have. When it ends, eternity begins! How is it being handled by you?

7

A HAPPY
FOREVER

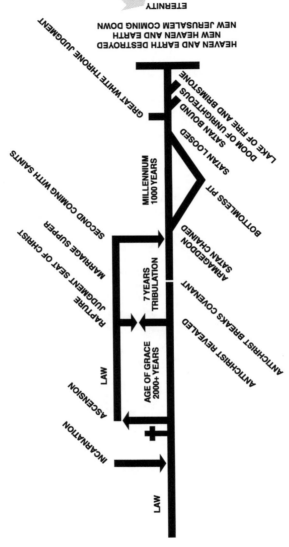

A NEW HEAVEN AND
A NEW EARTH

*And I saw a new heaven and a new earth; for the first
heaven and the first earth were passed away.*

Revelation 21:1

The judgment is past, time is no more, eternity has
begun. The world has shifted into its third and final
phase, all three of which have attention drawn to them
by the apostle Peter in his second epistle (II Pet. 3:5-7,
13). The reference is to a world that was, one that is and
another that is to be.

We naturally are most familiar with the world that is
by virtue of experience. But what about the world that
was? And more important, the world that is to come?

For that world that was, evidence is found. Not only is
this presented in the Word of God but it is also confirmed
in our present world. You see, Scripture records that judgment climaxed the world that was and this present world
bears ample manifestation of that judgment. The scars
of a past cataclysmic experience are found in many places
of our present world. It is most reasonable to believe
that the cataclysm experienced was the flood of Noah's

day. While the Scripture does not offer an abundance of information regarding that world of the past, one fact is recorded—God judged it! And it is well to note the reason—he judged it because of sin (Gen. 6:5-7)!

The apostle Peter makes reference to the world of the past for a basic purpose. Scoffers, he tells us, will arrive on the scene nearing the end of this present world. Their premise will be that the world goes on—that the coming of Christ and his judgment of this present world are sheer fantasy. He nails down the fact, however, that just as surely as God destroyed one world in the past, so he will destroy another—this present one! He then goes on to tell how it will happen (II Pet. 3).

Understanding Peter's account doesn't take a great deal of imagination for those who, like the author, have lived through the era of World War II wherein was witnessed that devastation and destruction of the atom bombs which were dropped on Hiroshima and Nagasaki. Especially is this true when we take into account that bombs and warheads possessed today are so vastly superior in destructive capability as to make the ones dropped on those cities appear as playthings by comparison.

Now, whether God will use man's own devices to bring about the destruction of our present world or accomplish such destruction by a fiat of his own is not known. What is known, however, is that "the heavens shall pass away with a great noise, and the elements shall melt with fervent heat; the earth also, and the works that are in it, shall be burned up" (II Pet. 3:10).

Peter's language is not vague in the context of that

which we understand today. A close examination of this text in its original would indicate that there is resident within this world the force capable to bring about its destruction (II Pet. 3:7). There is further the suggestion of an unloosing of the atoms, the basic building blocks of our universe (II Pet. 3:10). But that's not all. The language of verse 12 in this epistle suggests a "wasting away" process to become a part of the total so as to make this earth uninhabitable. This could conceivably be radio-active fallout in the context of what we know today.

We can only speculate what it all means in terms of that which we know. But suffice it to say that this present world is destined for a tragic ending. No amount of moral, social, behavioral or any other applied science will alter, change or stall the inevitable. Remember the thrust of Scripture here and elsewhere also is that just as surely as one world in the past has experienced the mighty judging hand of God upon it, just as surely is that inevitable, God-decreed judgment pending for this present world.

There is yet another world. Not only do we find reference to it here in Peter's epistle, but in numerous other Scriptures. It is a world yet future as distinguished from the world that was and the world that is. It is not a fantasy or a dream world but one equally as real as both worlds before it.

The world that is today is essentially the one that was. Will the one that is to come be essentially the same world that has undergone the judgment of God a second time? It is here where opinions vary. Those who have examined the Scriptures are divided. Some suggest a brand new world to replace the old and others suggest a renovated one. No amount of speculation will settle the issue this side of that world to come. We shall wait and see.

There is, however, in my opinion much to be said in favor of a totally new world replacing the one that was and now is. Foremost is the very essence of the language describing that future world. We are informed that it consists of "new heavens and a new earth" and also a "new Jerusalem" (II Pet. 3:13; Rev. 21:1-2). Taking a literal approach it is certainly most logical to believe that "new" means exactly that—new, brand new! In application of such logic, if we were to buy something sold as "new" and then find after that it was something old done over or used before, there is little question as to our reaction. And so, we would conceive God to perform in like manner in the keeping of his own Word.

We have already stated that this new world is not one of fantasy or dream but real and literal. In telling us about the Holy City, the New Jerusalem, materials mentioned are gold, pearls and costly stones. Why the mention of such literal materials known to us if they indeed are not literal.

It would appear that the world to be will have only one city—the New Jerusalem. As to the size of that world we may only conjecture. Its city, however, evidencing the marks of exquisite, divine architecture in the form of a cube will be 1,500 miles square (Rev. 21:16). It is most difficult, in fact impossible, to imagine such a city, even considering any of the cities of this present world that bear the marks of the best in city planning. To say the least, it will be a beautiful city and our experience then will probably make that to be the understatement of time.

Where are the great empires of the past and those great cities that marked their glory—Nineveh, Babylon, Ephesus? One commenting on this put it well, "wild beasts now roam those grounds where once their proud temples reigned." Not so with the new city—it is a "forever city," according to the Hebrew writer who states, "For here have we no continuing city, but we seek one to come" (Heb. 13:14).

In this world we are concerned about where to live. As water seeks its level so we are prone to be selective not only in the matter of residence but also certainly in association. A select society resides in that coming world—so select that this world's majority, by far, would be most uncomfortable should it inherit the world to come. Have no fear, it won't! John, the Beloved, tells us who will not be there, "But the fearful, and unbelieving, and the abominable, and murderers, and fornicators, and sorcerers, and idolaters, and all liars, shall have their part in the lake which burneth with fire and brimstone, which is the second death" (Rev. 21:8). Read the list again and ponder for a moment how select this new world's society will really be. It will be composed only of the redeemed of all the ages. This select company will be there because of a relationship established with God in this life—a relationship based on a personal faith in Jesus Christ (John 14:6; Eph. 2:8, 9).

In conclusion, our logical concern should not be with the world that was—about which our knowledge is relatively limited—nor with the world that now is—one most real to us by virtue of experience. But rather, our concern should be with that world that is yet to come and especially so because of the fate that is decreed for this present world (I John 2:14, 15). For which world are you living now?

8

IT'S STRICTLY PERSONAL

IT'S STRICTLY PERSONAL

*So then every one of us shall give
an account of himself to God.*

God has a program for this world. I have presented the major events of that program in their sequence. Many of these are yet future. Judging by what is transpiring, that future is upon us. God's program moves rapidly toward its predicted climax.

In PUTTING IT ALL TOGETHER one fact stands out: you and I are involved! And there is no way to shrug off such involvement. How we respond is of tremendous import both to God and to us—to him because of his great love, to us because of the eternal consequences.

Two options obtain: we may either respond to God's love or we may reject that love and go our own way. It's up to us—IT'S STRICTLY PERSONAL (John 3:16-18).

God's great love centers in the person and work of the Lord Jesus Christ. This has been presented throughout but especially in Chapter 1.

John, in his Gospel, records Christ's own words: "For God so loved the world, that he gave his only begotten

Son, that whosoever believeth in him should not perish, but have everlasting life" (John 3:16). Paul, the apostle, puts it this way: "But God commendeth his love toward us in that, while we were yet sinners, Christ died for us" (Rom. 5:8).

God loved us so much that he sent Christ to die for us. It was necessary because we are sinners, a fact that we don't like to admit but is nevertheless true. This fact is established by both our nature and our experience.

Now, let's put it all together as far as we're concerned. To respond to his love involves agreeing with God. We must agree with him about ourselves—that we are indeed sinners. Then we must agree with him about Christ—that he was God in the flesh, died for us—for our sins—was buried and rose again. Frankly, that he was everything he claimed to be. And finally, we must personally invite him into our lives to become our very own Savior and Lord. That's what "believing on him" really is all about. This is more than a mere mental act. It involves the heart. It is an act of surrender. And IT'S STRICTLY PERSONAL!

You may do this right now. Simply tell God that you agree with him about yourself and about Christ. Then ask Christ to become your personal Savior and Lord. If you do this sincerely, you will understand and experience what I really mean when I say, "IT'S STRICTLY PERSONAL" (Rom. 3:23; 6:23; John 1:12; Rom. 10:9-10, 13; Eph. 2:8-9).

ABOUT THE AUTHOR

Harold Nickel's involvement in Christian ministry, along with his wife, began more than 67 years ago. He has served as a pastor, church planter, missionary, Biblical counselor and seminar speaker. While a great majority of this ministry has been in the U.S., it has also taken him to foreign countries, including the continent of Australia for more than 10 years. It was there, through a series of God-ordained events, that his life was radically impacted, leading to a full time career in biblical counseling. As an outgrowth of his professional counseling, a seminar ministry called Focus For Living was developed. This ministry has taken him across the continent, serving numerous churches in recent years. The Nickels are now retired but he is frequently invited to preach and present the occasional seminar.

Made in the USA
San Bernardino, CA
04 November 2015